Villager Jim's

Moorland Wildlife

I dedicate this book to my great chum, John Nicholson. When my wife Jo and I moved from the big city to the countryside, we met John and his wife, Liz, and we all instantly became friends. John is an avid wildlife enthusiast and has spent his life learning about the animals in and around the Peak District. Over the years, he has inspired me, telling me, for instance, about the butterfly that just landed or that the green woodpecker will only eat ants that are prominent in local woodlands. John and I often bump into each other at dawn with our cameras, and chat about what we have seen that morning, passing on any new places discovered or animals seen for the first time in different locations. Without his help and enthusiasm, I don't think I would have fallen in love with the outdoors in the way that I have. So this book is a way of saying thank you to John for sharing his passion for wildlife, which is reflected in the pictures I take with my camera every day.

Villager Jim's
Moorland Wildlife

WHITE OWL

First published in Great Britain in 2017 by
PEN & SWORD WHITE OWL
an imprint of
Pen & Sword Books Ltd
47 Church Street
Barnsley
South Yorkshire
S70 2AS

Copyright © Villager Jim 2017

ISBN 978 1 5267 0675 1

Printed and bound in India by Replika Press Pvt. Ltd.

Pen & Sword Books Ltd incorporates the imprints of Pen & Sword Archaeology, Atlas, Aviation, Battleground,
Discovery, Family History, History, Maritime, Military, Naval, Politics, Railways, Select, Transport, True Crime, and
Fiction, Frontline Books, Leo Cooper, Praetorian Press, Seaforth Publishing, Wharncliffe and White Owl.

For a complete list of Pen & Sword titles please contact:
PEN & SWORD BOOKS LIMITED
47 Church Street, Barnsley, South Yorkshire, S70 2AS, England
E-mail: enquiries@pen-and-sword.co.uk
Website: www.pen-and-sword.co.uk

Introduction

If ever there was a job worth getting up for in the morning, being a wildlife photographer is top of the list for me. What started as a hobby after a move from city life to the countryside has developed into the best new career imaginable, and I wouldn't change it for anything.

Living in the heart of the Peak District, I am spoiled on a daily basis by what Nature gives. From sweeping barren moorlands to well-managed fields and country lanes teeming with wildlife, the landscapes are wonderfully diverse, offering distinctive scenes and moods with each season. My journeys with my camera encompass them all.

I go out always an hour before dawn. Of course, that is a different time every day: in early summer it is around 4.00 am and in the bleak midwinter, around 7.00 am. The weather can change very quickly at any time of year, and when Nature throws her worst at you, some of the best photographic opportunities often open up. Rolling mists are always exciting, and when I spot wildlife in their midst, that is a bonus. I learnt very early on to endure all weathers – having a good coat and warm gloves certainly helps. The day I don't go out may be the day that I miss a spectacular opportunity. My most famous image of all – *The Ascent of Stag* – was taken in murky, drizzly and foggy conditions. I had nearly decided not to go that day as it seemed a bit pointless, but oh my goodness, did I nearly miss

out! Those moments don't give two hoots about the weather.

I never know what I'm going to come across, and that is the huge joy of it. I don't go out with a particular shot in mind; I can't work like that. I need to be free to seize the day and whatever presents itself in front of me. People adore my pictures of Highland cows; they always get great reactions on social media. Deer, and particularly stags, are also a stunning sight; to catch them you really have to be around at dawn, as with foxes and badgers. In fact, most wildlife is up and about way earlier than we humans are and tends to fade away when we start bustling around. You can often witness the end of an owl's night out. Tawnys and barn owls usually hunt during the hours of darkness so it is always a pleasure to catch sight of them flying up and down drystone walls looking for prey.

There are lots of special moments throughout the year, but spring has to be my favourite season. I relish seeing the first curlews arrive across the fields along with their haunting calls. I enjoy the first signs of animals pairing up, like the two little owls who sit side by side in a ruined barn a mile away from my home. Seeing them perched together inside the old window frame is a sight I never tire of. The optimism of spring arrives with the crocuses and daffodils, and then the lambs are out in the fields in some places. As springtime progresses, the season's energy and warmth sees off the coldness of winter and wildlife becomes more visible.

Over time, I have become familiar with the different traits of the animals I observe. It helps enormously that I know what they are likely to do when I'm preparing for a shot. For example, when male ducks are looking to pair up with a mate they will push their body and head under the water, showing off to the females. When they leave the water after this they will stand tall and flap their wings out to get clean and dry. If you are ready for this, you can get cracking pictures of them with their wings spread wide like an angel. A hare, when caught out in the open and has frozen to the spot, will always lower its ears and wait for you to move. If you stay stock still with your eyes locked on, it will stay put, but the moment you dip your eyes, they go POW! Having this knowledge gains you valuable seconds; if you lock the focus and move your eyes down they will bolt … but then you get the action shot! Having the ability to 'control' a wild animal in this way always amazes me.

Spontaneity is the real key to my photography. Most of my pictures are taken on the spur of the moment. I don't sit around and wait, but I do know how to grab the best shots from those fabulous two- or three-second opportunities. Many is the time I have been out with colleagues and, like in the old Wild West, I have seen something, drawn my camera, taken three shots and lowered it before my pals have even spotted what it is I am shooting. Being quick on the draw is a really great thing to help a photographer grab special moments. They don't tend to wait for you!

A fellow photographer and I now run courses to teach all the techniques of better photography, and these have proved very popular. You can save yourself months of time by getting good advice that is easy to follow. Having this basic knowledge can inspire you to go out and practice and soon achieve great results. Gaining experience will soon reward with good composition, colour and tone. It can prove very addictive. Some of my most dramatic photographs are silhouettes, which are often very powerful and emotive. I love taking shots where the light source is behind the subject.

However well prepared you are, there is always an amount of luck involved in getting that special picture. *The Ascent of Stag* remains my luckiest shot to date, with six stags walking away from me over the brow of a hill in the early morning, equidistant apart and ascending in size from left to right – a one in 10 million shot! On a more domestic note, I recently took a photograph of my pooch Barnaby when my daughter had just thrown him a biscuit. I managed to capture the very moment his eyes locked onto the target before it disappeared down his throat. *After the Walk* – a photo of my black Labrador Dilly asleep on one of our leather chairs – is perhaps the most famous image I've ever taken. It has been seen all over the world on social media, and has literally changed my life.

I have won the South West News Service Press Photographer of the Year for two years running, which has never been done before, and I was lucky enough to win editor's choice in the British Wildlife Photography Awards 2014. Of course, getting that special shot is reward enough in itself, but sharing the results with others is part of what makes this job so enjoyable.

Villager Jim

Visit Villager Jim's Facebook page at **www.facebook.com/villagerjim**
And his website at **www.villagerjim.com**

Sunrise in the Peaks.

Red kite - a stunning bird of prey.

Perfect grace and agility, and a wingspan that can extend to 5½ feet.

Dancing in the wind.

A natural scavenger – the piece of ham in this opportunist's claws was part of someone's picnic just a few moments earlier!

The red kite's red/orange body, forked tail and banded feathers of black, brown and white are so distinctive from below.

A tender moment, when velvet-covered antlers are starting to grow.

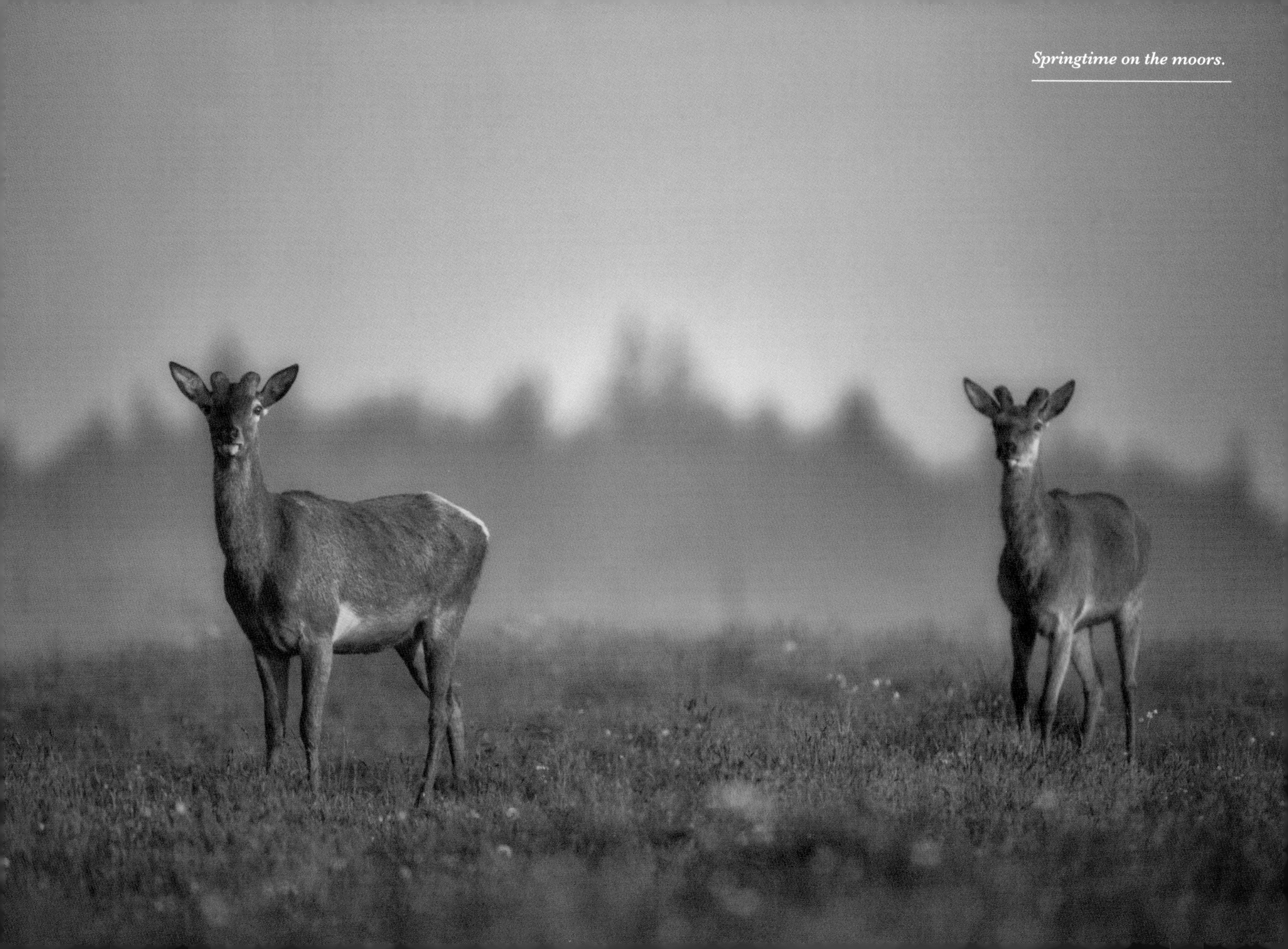

Springtime on the moors.

Perfect colour matching: the red and buff tones of the moorland grasses allow some cover for the roaming deer.

I beg your pardon; are you following me?

Caught in the garden! This stag is surveying a rather more manicured landscape than he usually frequents.

Those sensitive ears perk up at the faintest of sounds, which is why I have to be so careful when stalking deer for a photo.

It is always lovely to spot a grey shrike - a rare but regular winter visitor to the UK. They like to survey open hunting ground from a perch, keeping a keen eye out for insects, small mammals and birds.

The grey shrike's distinctive black mask and pearl grey plumage prove that you don't have to be colourful to be beautiful.

Winter branches are a perfect perch from which to view the landscape.

Stoats are well known for their curiosity, but this one nevertheless looks rather surprised to see a man with a camera standing right in front of him.

A family of young kits practise their agility skills in the warm sunshine.

Those black-tipped tails are perfect for a game of follow-my-leader!

Phileas Pheasant feels right at home in the open moorland and woodland edges of the Peak District.

*The closer you get to a pheasant,
the more their rich and shimmering
colours become apparent.*

Perched on a gate, passing the time of day, this male pheasant is blissfully unaware that his species is one of the most hunted in the world!

At Pilsley crown court today, the three judges sentenced Derek to life for his part in the Great Grain Robbery. Derek walked out of the court (bottom right) with his head held low, contemplating a very beak future ...

A male pheasant resplendent in his deep chestnut and golden plumage tipped with white and black, rich green-blue iridescent head, tufted ears and bright red wattle.

Spring is here ... and testosterone levels are rising!

Kung fu pheasants - anything to impress the ladies!

*Jeepers Jim, at least give
me time to strike a pose!*

Making pheasant shapes against the setting sun.

Adders are not something you expect to see very often in the Peak District, but they are more common than you would think.

A male adder from the eastern moors, spotted in early spring.

A young kestrel bathed in the gentle spring light of Beeley Moor.

Kestrels regularly hover over fields, often in the wake of farm vehicles.

Lock on! The kestrel's eyesight is extremely keen, even in poor light.

A grub makes a small but tasty meal.

Kestrels can be seen hunting from static perches in the winter.

The short-eared owl loves open moorland, its broad wings allowing it to soar and swoop in silence.

Looking out from the edge of Shillito Wood, near Ramsey Moor in the Peak District National Park. A walk in this area will usually reward with the sight of these beautiful deer, as well as some spectacular scenery.

Fistycuffs at dawn.

Shoulder-deep in the spring meadow.

The deer often come to the edge of the moor for a morning's graze.

Three beautiful young red deer leap over an old fence up on the moors; something you can only really get to see around dawn as they tend to slink away to the woods during the day.

*Shhh ... walls have ears,
don't you know!*

Hares amongst the buttercups.

Harry and the grey dawn.

This open farmland is perfect for hares to forage, relying on their acute hearing and fast running speed to evade predators.

Hares spend a lot of time atop walls; I'm guessing it allows for great all-round viewing!

A smart hare, with his back to the wall for safety.

One of my greatest pleasures of all is spotting a fox in the early morning, before the world wakes up.

Basking in the spring sunshine.

*Baa, baa black sheep,
have you any wool?*

'Wait, Lance, how the hell did you get up?'

Boys and girls, stand up straight – and say cheese for Jim!

Playing leapfrog.

Now that's what you really call a spring lamb!

A beautiful day ahead, if the sunrise fulfills its promise.

My horses against a stunning red dawn.

Pied wagtails doing a mating dance, which is quite elaborate for a small, usually modest bird.

Pied wagtail with dinner for her young.

*A gull with rather
angelic wings.*

Woods are magical places at dawn.

'If we're spotted, guys, just say
we came to view the house!'

A one-in-a-million shot, taken early morning at Chatsworth. What are the odds of a line of stags coming towards you in ascending height?

A rolling mist near Curbar.

The unmistakable curlew, with long, slender legs, and downward curved bill, set against a stunning red dawn on the moors.

A curlew over Chatsworth. They are a surprisingly large bird when they take off, with a massive swooshing wingspan.

Spring and summer are great seasons to catch a glimpse of the curlew in the Peak District.

Looking for worms amongst the buttercups.

*A perfect spot for a
morning chinwag.*

Resting a leg and
waiting for the dawn.
_____

Lift-off! The curlew's haunting cry can often be heard across the silent farmland and moors.

Curlew on the rocks ... sounds like a cocktail, doesn't it?

Work it girlfriend, work it!
Baby curlews go for a walk
along my favourite lane.

*The partridge family
meander up the lane.*

A lapwing arrives on the moor ready for the spring/summer breeding season.

Lapwing with two very very cute babies. They nest in small scrapes in the ground in open landscape, so they can see their predators at a distance.

'I am the greatest!'
thought Harry.
—————

A hare enjoying the lush fields of summer.
—————

Hares love tender grass shoots - one of their main sources of food, along with cereal crops.

A field in common share
A partridge and a hare ...

Breakfast is served! Tree pipits are rare but can be seen in the Peak District from mid-April until the time of their migration back to Saharan Africa in August/September. They love the woodland/moorland boundaries.

A meadow pipit often looks for a convenient post and loves the open moorland of Derbyshire in summertime.

A wheatear on a post. Another summer visitor that seems to enjoy the open moorland, and returns to Africa after the breeding season.

A wheatear on his own miniature cliff edge.

A wheatear strikes a pose in the summer sunshine.

A little owl on a moorland post. This miniature of the owl species is more often spotted in daylight than its larger cousins.

Short-eared owl in the golden dawn of midwinter. This medium-sized owl can also be spotted hunting in the daytime.

This short-eared owl kindly turned its head for me, so I could see in more detail one of its distinctive yellow-orange eyes, circled by black rings and a mask of white.

———————————————

Catching this short-eared owl sitting on a post early one spring morning was a highlight of my photography year. It was one of those rare shots that make this photography malarkey so addictive.

Meadow pipit on a field post. They like the diverse habitats of the Peak District, especially in the breeding season.

A stunning rainbow over Abney and the hills beyond.

For those who have time to stand and stare, even a passing gull can add interest to the day.

Scooby snack: this hare's eyes are definitely bigger than its belly!

Just look at those ears. If they are pointing at you, you have been noticed! A deer's sense of smell is also very acute, alerting it to any unusual goings-on.

Yo Jim, I just did my job to perfection, so the boss says I'm allowed some swagger time!

Do I get a biscuit now?

*A truly wild stag leaps a
drystone wall near Curbar.*

The gentle afternoon sun catches this stag's antlers, giving them a golden appearance.

In many species of deer, the antlers increase in size each year, reaching their maximum at full maturity. These look as if they could be made of bronze!

Master of all he surveys.

Watch my back, Bob!

A good old strut sure gets the ladies going.

About as good a moment as it gets: the moors, a mist, a stag ... and no humans for miles.

Nobility amidst the purple heather.

OK, Jim, how do I look?

Moorland gathering.

An early morning sea of yellow cascades over the hills.

Ringed plovers are coastal birds but in the Peak District, they are attracted to the heath and heather moorlands, as well as old gravel pits, which now offer marsh and reed beds.

Jamie playing James Bond, talking into his watch.

A typical pose for a grey squirrel, with its magnificent bushy tail arched over its back.

Dan's table manners were constantly letting him down.

Milo seems pretty chuffed with his birdseed find!

A fluffball amongst the heather.

My local farmers, Peter and Linda, live atop the Longstone Moor, and even though it is very bleak, their sheep always look in tip-top condition.

If Norma can keep it together and not move a muscle, she feels certain she won't be seen.

Posing in the heather.

It had been a party night to remember!

Once rare in the UK, common buzzards have been steadily growing in number. Their aerial acrobatics are impressive, but they can also hunt from a perch – or perhaps this one is just taking time out.

A magical starling moment for me as a few hundred thousand come together to make the shape of a flying bird.

Spot the peregrine amongst the starlings!

A balloon-shaped flock of starlings coming home at sunset, with two peregrine falcons in hot pursuit.

Pheasants can get very territorial, and this can result in a ferocious flurry of feathers and claws.

Pheasants are competitive during the mating season and can mate with more than one female ... leaving her to do all the hard work afterwards, of course!

A jackdaw leaping over the rising sun.

A gorgeous moorland winter scene, which is as cold as it looks.

A blanket of snow covering the hills behind Foolow.

The limestone hamlet of Foolow on a winter's day, set against the rolling hills of the Peak District.

The historic Barrell Inn, at the head of Bretton Clough, looking glorious on top of the snowy peaks.

A healthy coat to withstand the worst that the weather can throw at it.

A Highland on the moors above Curbar.

Curly horned Swaledales feel right at home in the Peak District.

Lone tree near Eyam.

A little owl, typically squat, with piercing green eyes. A fence post makes a good perch during its nighttime and early dawn hunting.

A barn owl starts his nighttime work.

This barn owl had just spotted his prey on the moor and looked like a bumble bee for a split second.

This barn owl made my year by coming in to land a staggering 15 feet away from me as I was taking pictures. One of life's great moments!

*Beautiful barn owls,
gliding through the air.*

Scouring the moorlands for prey, this
short-eared owl's flight is so graceful.

*Ghostly beauty and absolute silence
as the barn owl hovers above its prey.*

After a few days of rain, a barn owl ventures out for food.

Dinner is about to be served.

The closer you get to a barn owl, the more their delicate colours impress.

*Low-flying barn owl
hovering above its prey.*

Laura the little owl on sentry duty.

A stunning little near Baslow.

*Take-off in the light of
a cold dawn.*

A startled pheasant making a quick exit, his breath visible in the cold air.

Its not that often you see a pheasant in a tree, but I managed to nab this chap near Hassop.

Undercarriage down ... a crow comes in to land.

The sunset and the crow.

A buzzard ready for its first hunt of the day.

A young buzzard.

Getting ready to soar.

A stunning buzzard at Bubnell.

The winter tree and the merlin – the UK's smallest bird of prey.

A wren singing her heart out on a winter bramble.

Greater spotted woodpecker from Shillito Woods.

A stunning yellowhammer on a field post; one of the prettiest of Peak District birds.

*Two stags and a doe blending
in with the moorland colours.*

A penny for his thoughts?

'Psst, Catherine! I told you I wasn't lying about the paparazzi coming after me.'

*Deer admiring the fantastic
Curbar view.*

Fifteen seconds of heart-pounding heavy breathing as we bump into each other in the woods (and that was just me!).

Does gathering in the snow.

Meeting a stag on the moors half an hour before dawn is a fantastic experience. This one was perhaps 20 metres away from me; I hadn't seen him, then he turned to walk away ...

Visit Villager Jim's website shop for a range of gifts and homeware featuring his wildlife photographs

- Greetings Cards
- Canvas Prints
- Calendars
- Books
- Jigsaw Puzzles

- Cushions
- Stationery
- Tablet Covers
- Home & Garden ware
- Luggage

- Mugs
- Phone Covers
- Clocks
- Candles
- Calenders

and much more ....

www.villagerjimsshop.com